Buddhist Temple

For Marc Neiderman

For a free color catalog describing Gareth Stevens' list of high-quality books and multimedia programs, call 1-800-542-2595 (USA) or 1-800-461-9120 (Canada). Gareth Stevens Publishing's Fax: (414) 225-0377.

Gareth Stevens Publishing thanks Reverend Tonen Sara O'Connor for her assistance with the accuracy of the text. Reverend O'Connor is a resident priest at Kokyo-an (Milwaukee Zen Center). She began studying Buddhism in 1982, took the precepts as a lay Buddhist in 1988, was ordained in 1994, and received Dharma Transmission from Rev. Tozen Akiyama in Japanese Soto Zen Buddhism in 1999. She has practiced at Toyama Nisodo, Shogoji Monastery, and Keisei Zendo in Japan; Zen Mountain Center (Yokoji) in California; and with Master Sheng-yen in New York state.

The Publisher recognizes that there is more than one Buddhist tradition. While all Buddhists have the same basic beliefs, there are several schools of Buddhist practice. This book tends to focus primarily on the Theravadan tradition, but references have been included to address other types of Buddhist practice in the Books, Videos, and Web Sites on pages 30 and 31.

Library of Congress Cataloging-in-Publication Data available upon request from publisher.
Fax: (414) 225-0377 for the attention of the Publishing Records Department.

ISBN 0-8368-2605-1

This North American edition first published in 2000 by
Gareth Stevens Publishing
1555 North RiverCenter Drive, Suite 201
Milwaukee, WI 53212 USA

Original edition © 1998 by Franklin Watts.
First published in 1998 by Franklin Watts,
96 Leonard Street, London EC2A 4RH, England.
This U. S. edition © 2000 by Gareth Stevens, Inc.
Additional end matter © 2000 by Gareth Stevens, Inc.

Editor: Samantha Armstrong
Series Designer: Kirstie Billingham
Illustrator: Gemini Patel
Religious Education Consultant: Margaret Barratt, Religious Education lecturer and author
Buddhist Consultant: Ronald Maddox, General Secretary, The Buddhist Society
Reading Consultant: Prue Goodwin, Reading and Language Information Centre, Reading

Gareth Stevens Series Editor: Dorothy L. Gibbs

Photographic acknowledgements:
Cover: Steve Shott Photography; Ann and Bury Peerless.
Inside: p. 6 Ann and Bury Peerless; p. 7 AKG; p. 9 Jean-Leo Dugast, Panos Pictures; p. 11 Jean-Leo Dugast, Panos Pictures; p. 17 Trip Photographic Library/B. Vikander; p. 20 Jim Holmes, Panos Pictures; p. 22 Dominic Sanson, Panos Pictures; p. 23 Christophe Bluntzer, Impact. All other photographs by Steve Shott Photography.

With thanks to Ven. Somaratana and everyone at the Thames Meditation Centre, Croydon.

Printed in the United States of America

1 2 3 4 5 6 7 8 9 04 03 02 01 00

PLACES OF WORSHIP

Buddhist Temple

Angela Wood

Gareth Stevens Publishing
MILWAUKEE

This symbol of the Noble Eightfold Path is
used to represent the Buddhist faith.

Contents

Words that appear in the glossary are printed in **boldface**
type the first time they occur in the text.

Temples around the World

A temple is a place where Buddhists go to learn about the teachings of the **Buddha**, to show respect for him, and to be with other Buddhists. There are Buddhist temples all around the world. Some of them are called **viharas**.

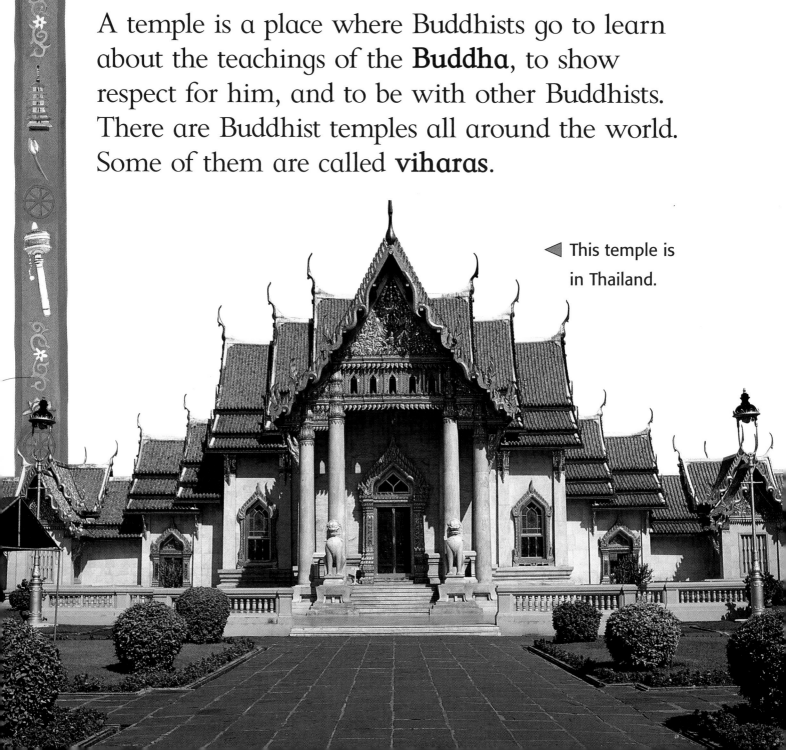

◁ This temple is in Thailand.

The Buddha Rupas

Buddhists follow the Buddha's teachings, but they do not worship him. Pictures or images of the Buddha are called **Buddha rupas**. They help Buddhists remember what the Buddha said and did.

The Buddha is shown ▷ in different positions, or **mudras**. Each mudra has a special meaning.

The Buddha

The Buddha was born a prince named Siddattha Gotama. He lived in a palace in Nepal. Siddattha had everything he could want, but he felt that there was more to know about life. So he went to see what life was like outside the palace. There he saw a sick man, an old man, and a dead man, and he realized that everyone shared the same problem as these three men. Everyone would suffer and die. Siddattha decided to find an answer to this problem.

Many temples have ▶ paintings showing stories from the Buddha's life. This painting shows the Buddha leaving the palace.

8

Understanding Life

Siddattha met holy men and tried living their strict and simple lives, but he did not find the answer to the problem. Then, one day, he decided to sit beneath a tree until he understood why people are unhappy and how they can be wise, peaceful, and happy.

When Siddattha realized the answer, he was **enlightened**. *Buddha* means "enlightened one," or "the one who knows."

The Buddha is sitting on a ▷ bed of lotus flowers. A lotus flower grows out of muddy water. The Buddha said that becoming "enlightened" was like growing from muddy water into the light.

Inside a Temple

Every Buddhist temple has a **shrine** inside, sometimes in a special room. The most important part of the shrine is the Buddha rupa. It is in the middle of the shrine and is raised high to show how special it is. Buddhists place offerings and other items all around the Buddha rupa.

Sometimes the shrine has a model of a pointed mound called a **stupa**. When the Buddha died, his ashes and some of his belongings were put inside a huge stupa. Now stupas contain reminders of the Buddha and Buddhist writings.

In this shrine, the Buddha ▷ is sitting beneath the bodhi tree where he was enlightened. A small stupa is in the corner.

The Three Jewels

The three ideas that are most important to Buddhists are called the **Three Jewels**. They are the Buddha, the **Dhamma**, and the **Sangha**, which is the Buddhist community.

◄ As these children make offerings in front of the Buddha rupa, they say the names of the Three Jewels.

The Dhamma

The Buddha's teachings are called the Dhamma. He believed that people cannot be happy if they think only about themselves and their belongings.

The Buddha said these four things about life. They are called the **Four Noble Truths**:

1. *There is unhappiness in life.*

2. *People are unhappy when they want to get only their own wishes.*

3. *There is a way to end this unhappiness.*

4. *The way to end unhappiness is called the **Noble Eightfold Path**. It shows people how to live wisely and happily.*

The Noble Eightfold Path

The **symbol** of the Noble Eightfold Path is a wheel with eight spokes. The Noble Eightfold Path is the Middle Way; it is not too easy and not too hard. It helps Buddhists be happy by seeing life clearly, doing good things, and making their minds peaceful.

This model of the Noble ▷ Eightfold Path is on top of a temple. The deer on each side of the model remind Buddhists of a speech the Buddha gave in a deer park.

Sangha

Sangha means all Buddhist **monks** and **nuns** everywhere. It can also mean the whole Buddhist community.

Just as the Buddha did, monks and nuns live a simple life away from their families. They **meditate**, teach the Dhamma, and help people. Some live this way their whole lives, others for only a short time.

Buddhist monks and ▶ nuns have very few possessions. They have a robe, a bowl, a belt, a razor, a needle, a water filter, a toothpick, and a walking stick.

Other members of the Buddhist community
thank the monks and nuns by giving them food
and, sometimes, robes. This giving is called **dana**.

Meditation

Meditation is a special kind of quiet thinking. When Buddhists meditate, their minds become clear and bright.

When Buddhists practice meditation, they kneel or sit cross-legged, sometimes on cushions, and relax. They sit quietly and very still, with their eyes closed or slightly open, and they breathe calmly. Some Buddhists say a verse or **mantra** over and over.

Buddhists meditate in the ▷ temple or at home. They meditate by themselves or with others.

◁ Zen Buddhists make special gardens to help them meditate. These gardens have rocks, raked sand or small stones, and maybe a few trees.

21

Puja

Some of the ways Buddhists show their **respect** for the Buddha are called **puja**. Buddhists sometimes sit or kneel with their shoes off in front of a shrine. With their heads bowed and the palms of their hands together, which is a position called **anjali**, they say a verse about the Three Jewels:

*"I go to the Buddha as my **refuge**.*

I go to the Dhamma as my refuge.

I go to the Sangha as my refuge."

Buddhists also offer flowers to the Buddha. The flowers die, showing that everything in life changes. Buddhists light candles because the Dhamma lights up the world. They burn **incense** because it has a sweet smell, like the sweetness of the Dhamma, that spreads into the world.

incense sticks ▷

◁ candle

Metta Sutta

The Metta Sutta are verses about loving kindness. They are often read or chanted at the end of puja. *Metta* means loving kindness, being peaceful, and caring for all living things. The Buddha said that everyone should have metta inside them.

◁ These flags in Tibet show metta being sent out to everyone and everything in the world.

▲ Buddhists in Tibet turn wheels
with mantras on them to send
goodness into the world.

A School in a Temple

Most Buddhist temples have classes for children in which they learn the Dhamma, often from a monk or a nun. They also learn how to meditate and how to lead a Buddhist life.

These children are ▶ learning about the Three Jewels.

▽ In the past, the Buddha's teachings, along with rules for monks and nuns, were written on narrow pieces of palm leaves that were threaded together into books.

Glossary

anjali (<u>ahn</u>-jah-lee): the sitting or kneeling position that shows respect for the Buddha.

Buddha: "enlightened one."

Buddha rupa (<u>Boo</u>-dah <u>roop</u>-ah): an image of the Buddha.

dana (<u>dah</u>-nah): giving monks and nuns food, clothing, and shelter.

Dhamma (<u>Dah</u>-mah): the teachings of the Buddha.

enlightened: seeing things clearly and wisely.

Four Noble Truths: what the Buddha taught about the suffering in life and how to end it.

incense: material that has a sweet, soothing smell when it is burned.

mantra (<u>mahn</u>-trah): a word or phrase repeated over and over to calm the mind.

meditate: to think in a special, quiet way that makes the mind clear and calm.

metta (<u>meh</u>-tah): loving kindness.

monks: men who leave their families to teach the Dhamma.

mudras (<u>moo</u>-drahs): the different and meaningful positions of the Buddha in Buddha rupas.

Noble Eightfold Path: the "Middle Way" to find peace and happiness.

nuns: women who leave their families to teach the Dhamma.

puja (poo-jah): a Buddhist word for showing respect; also, the name of a service to show respect for the Buddha.

refuge: a place of safety, shelter, and protection.

respect: thoughtful and honorable consideration and treatment.

Sangha (Song-ah): all Buddhist monks and nuns; can also mean all followers of Buddhism.

shrine: a special place with a Buddha rupa in the center surrounded by offerings.

stupa (stoop-ah): a pointed, domelike structure, usually part of a shrine, with reminders of the Buddha inside.

symbol: an object or sign that stands for something else, such as an idea or another object.

Three Jewels: the Buddha, the Dhamma, and the Sangha.

vihara (vee-hah-rah): the place monks and nuns live; the word for some Buddhist temples.

29

More Books to Read

Buddha. Susan L. Roth (Delacorte Press)

Buddha Stories. Demi (Henry Holt & Company)

Buddhist. Beliefs and Cultures (series). Anita Ganeri (Children's Press)

Buddhist Festivals. Celebrate (series). Clive and Jane Erricker (Heineman Library)

Learning from the Dalai Lama: Secrets of the Wheel of Time. Karen Pandell and Barry Bryant (Dutton Children's Books)

The Little Lama of Tibet. Lois Raimondo (Scholastic)

One Hand Clapping. Rafe Martin (St. Martin's Press)

Sacred Myths: Stories of World Religions. Marilyn McFarlane (Sibyl)

Vietnam. Festivals of the World (series). Susan McKay (Gareth Stevens)

What Do We Know About Buddhism? What Do We Know About...? (series). Anita Ganeri (Peter Bedrick Books)

The Wisdom of the Crows and Other Buddhist Tales. Sherab Chodzin and Alexandra Kohn (Tricycle Press)

Videos

Buddhism and Black Belts. (Maryknoll World Productions)

Buddhism Comes to America. (Wishing Well Video)

Dalai Lama: The Soul of Tibet. (Library Video)

Zen: In Search of Enlightenment. (Palisades Home Video)

Web Sites

Buddha's Art of Healing
www2.lhric.org/pocantico/ tibet/tibet.htm

Buddhism in a Nutshell
www.tunglinkok.ca/ 9602/sources/teach.htm

Essentials of Buddhism
home.earthlink.net/ ~srama/index.html

The Life of Gotama Buddha
www.serve.com/cmtan/ LifeBuddha/buddha.htm

To find additional web sites, use a reliable search engine with one or more of the following keywords: *Buddha, Buddhism, Dalai Lama, Dhamma, mantras, meditation, mudras, Noble Eightfold Path, Siddattha Gotama, Tibet,* and *viharas.*

Index